SHIPWRECK
The Loss *of the*
Metta Catharina in 1786

by Ian Skelton

The loss of the *Metta Catharina*: an ordinary ship, an extraordinary story.

Jon Parlour

Front cover:
John Greep
recovering a bundle
of hides from the
cargo hold.
Photo. Colin Hannaford.

Back cover:
Colin Hannaford
recovering a wine
bottle from the
cookhouse area.
Photo. Mike Evans.

Acknowledgements

Particular thanks are due to His Royal Highness Prince Charles, Duke of Cornwall, for generously allowing the members of the Nautical Archaeology Section to work on the wreck-site. Thanks also to Dr Jonathan Adams; Dr Polydora Baker, English Heritage; Cdr Alan Bax; Ian Berry and his Team at Mount Edgcumbe House and Country Park, Torpoint, Cornwall; the staff at the Diving Diseases and Research Centre, Plymouth; the City of Plymouth Museums & Art Gallery; G. J. Cleverley, Bespoke Shoemakers, Old Bond Street, London; Dr Gloria Clifton, Royal Observatory, Greenwich; Heather Coleman, Dawnmist Studio, Exeter; Comp-air Construction & Mining Ltd; Camborne, Cornwall; Gordon Crocker, Chairman of the Friends of Mount Edgcumbe Country Park, Torpoint, Cornwall;

Paul Dart (Team member & Recruitment Officer); Mike Evans, (Senior Diver and *Metta Catharina* Trustee); The Flensburger Schiffahrtsmuseum und Verein Zur Förderung Des Flensburger Schiffahrtsmuseums; Colin Hannaford, (Deputy Team Leader and *Metta Catharina* Trustee); The Heritage Lottery Fund; Peter Holt, Sonardyne International, Plymouth; Dr A. E. W. Miles, Royal College of Surgeons; New & Lingwood Ltd; Bespoke Shoemakers, Jermyn Street, London;

Jon Parlour, (Team member and *Metta Catharina* Trustee); The Plymouth Sound Branch (164) of the British Sub-Aqua Club; Divers from Plymouth University Branch (474) of the British Sub-Aqua Club; The Sail Training Association for the use of the sail training ship 'The Hardiesse' in photographing leatherwork; Evelyn Skelton, (Volunteer to the *Metta Catharina* Trust); Virginia Smithson, Department of Medieval & Later Antiquities, The British Museum; Robin & Gill Snelson of the Russia Hide Company, Mylor, Cornwall and to the late Mike Viney, Technical Director, Marine Projects, Plymouth, without whose generous assistance the project could not have stayed afloat.

The members of the Nautical Archaeology Section of Plymouth Sound Branch of the British Sub-Aqua Club thank everyone who has helped them during their 32 years of work on this challenging underwater project. Regrettably space does not allow an acknowledgement to all our helpers and well-wishers, but it must be recorded here that without their generous help and encouragement, the task of surveying and excavating the wreck of the *Metta Catharina* would not have been possible.

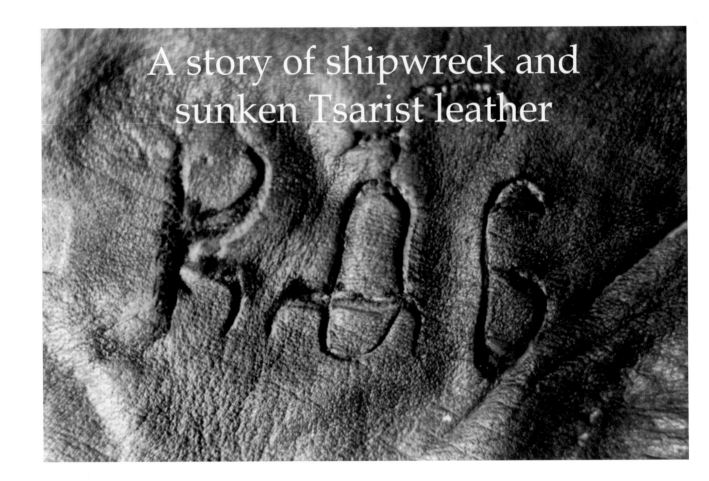

A story of shipwreck and sunken Tsarist leather

CONTENTS

'On land, or underwater, archaeological survey and excavation is labour intensive. Since on all underwater sites the work is done by divers, success or failure depends on their capabilities.'

Keith W. Muckelroy (1951 - 1980)

The north-west prospect of Plymouth Sound from Firestone Bay. Below the green slopes of Mount Edgcumbe Park are the Raven's Cliffs beneath which now stands the white Ravenness Point navigational beacon. To the left lies the western entrance to the English Channel. To the right lies the entrance to the Hamoaze. *Photo. Ian Skelton.*

Prologue

Feet firmly braced on the pitching deck, Captain Hans Twedt watched anxiously in the fading light as a sullen green swell collided with the bow of his ship. A curtain of spray swept the foredeck, followed by a low tremor in the hull. After leaving the port of St Petersburg barely a week before, with a cargo of hemp and 'Russia Calf' leather, his two-masted Danish brigantine, *Die Frau Metta Catharina von Flensburg*, had already had a long voyage. She had worked her way through the Gulf of Finland, across the Baltic, then out of the Kattegat around the top of Denmark, through the Skagerrak and out into the North Sea, all without incident. She had then passed through the Straits of Dover and out into the English Channel where the December weather now appeared to be taking a turn for the worse.

He left the deck for the warmth and shelter of the cookhouse where a glance at the barometer confirmed his growing fears: the weather was set to worsen and by nightfall he and his crew of six would be battling against a sou'westerly gale. The chart of the south coast of England, pinned to the table offered just one option for safety; Plymouth Sound, just four leagues distant. He reckoned that, anchored close under the Raven's Cliffs of Mount Edgcumbe, the ship would enjoy some protection from the savagery of the wind. He marked a course on the chart and then moved to join his crew.

After rounding Wembury Point the *Metta Catharina* beat her way across Plymouth Sound and hove to close to the Cornish shoreline. In the gathering darkness her best anchor was lowered, and her sails were furled. There would be no rest this night, but Hans felt comforted by the glow of lights which shone warmly from the big house on the hill above. He had cause to believe he had chosen a safe refuge. The Raven's Cliffs would provide shelter from the worst of any south-westerly blow. As the night wore on the strength of the wind increased. By 10 o'clock a full gale was howling into the Sound. The brigantine snubbed hard at her anchor rope as she rose and fell in the steep swells.

Past midnight the gale veered to the south-south-west and then fatefully full south. The ship was now pounded by heavy seas, which rushed unhindered into the previously safe mooring. Her anchor began to drag through its bed of loose sand as the swells gradually pushed the brigantine towards a dangerous underwater reef, known locally as the Bridge. Reaching shoal water, while still dragging to leeward, the *Metta Catharina* was soon within the surf zone. Hans, screaming to be heard above the roar of the wind, ordered the crew to hack off both masts. This desperate act with axe and hatchet was normal practice when a vessel was in danger of being driven aground. It prevented the mast's leverage from tearing the hull apart.

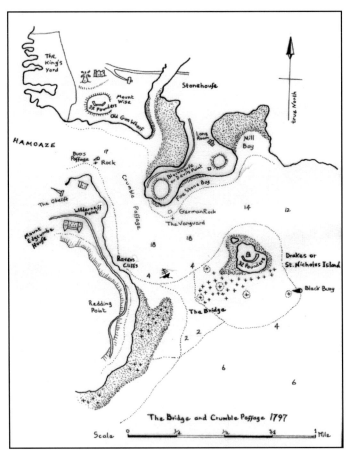

From an 18th century chart of Plymouth Sound. The location of the *Metta Catharina* has been marked.
Drawing by Wilf Jenkin and Ian Skelton.

Despite the courageous actions of the Danish mariners their ship was doomed. A train of towering breakers, formed by steep swells surging over the submerged reef, delivered the final death blow. They forced the ship into a violent plunge across the rock strewn ledge, which tore away her rudder, crushed her ribs and broke her back. With water cascading through gaping breaks in the hull and with one pump out of action Hans gave the order to abandon ship. As the crew struggled to launch a small cutter, they were offered some respite from the breaking waves when the *Metta Catharina* suddenly shed ballast through a hole in her side. This reduced her weight and allowed her passage over the 'hogs back' of the Bridge reef and into deeper, slightly less turbulent waters. Shortly afterwards, when sat hunched in the cutter, with his crew pulling strongly for the Hamoaze, Hans thought he could still hear the mournful tolling of his ship's bell. But when he strained to listen against the din of wind and wave there was nothing. The bell was silent.

In the early hours of the morning, at a welcoming tavern in the nearby town of Stonehouse, Captain Twedt and his crew discovered that they were not the only casualties of the gale. The *Christian Hendrick*, from Rotterdam with wheat and cheese for Barcelona, had also entered Plymouth Sound for shelter and been wrecked in the Cattewater. Local gossip proclaimed that the gale was the worst experienced in 1786. Nevertheless, this was small consolation for Hans, because at daybreak there was no sign of his brigantine. The trim vessel, just four years old, which carried the name of his beloved wife, had sunk without trace somewhere beneath the cliffs of Mount Edgcumbe Park.

Days later, when the winds had abated and the seas calmed, local fishermen tried their hands at grappling for gear and goods from the sunken ship. This age-old habit succeeded in recovering a mess of cordage, some bales of hemp and a few spars from the rigging, but little else. The heavy iron grapnels pulled the deckhouse and galley apart, scattering scores of firebricks from the hearth all around the splintered stump of the mainmast. They also tore the handles from the ship's pumps. But the valuable 'Russia Calf' leather, stowed securely below decks, remained stubbornly out of reach. The fishermen eventually lost interest, the story of the shipwreck was soon forgotten and the Danish brigantine *Die Frau Metta Catharina von Flensburg* faded into obscurity.

ONE
No safe haven

The mouth of Plymouth Sound stretches four nautical miles, from Wembury Point in Devon to Penlee Point in Cornwall. Its broad gape offers a reassuring break in an otherwise treacherous coastline. A sunken prehistoric gorge, or ria, the Sound has been a busy port since Bronze Age times. But Plymouth Sound had one serious disadvantage: when the wind blew from the south or south-east it became the much feared lee shore. It is believed that over the centuries as many as a thousand vessels, large and small, merchantmen and men-of-war alike, foundered, or were dashed to pieces on the rocks and reefs of this deceptively safe anchorage. In September 1691, with the wind blowing hard from the south, part of a large naval squadron came to grief near Wilderness Point, beneath Mount Edgcumbe. One of them, a ship of seventy guns, was wrecked and lost along with 420 sailors and marines. In January 1762 six merchantmen were lost and six men-of-war dismasted during a southerly gale elsewhere in the Sound. It was not until the breakwater was completed in 1841 that Plymouth Sound could be considered a safe anchorage.

The brigantine *Zephirus fra Flensburg*, 1804. The *Metta Catharina* would have looked much like this.
By kind permission of the Flensburg Shipping Museum.

In 1973 a Plymouth team of amateur underwater archaeologists decided to investigate the shipwreck resources of a chosen area of the Sound. Their aim was to whet the appetite of the public and the museum authorities towards sunken history by providing them with interesting material recovered from long-lost ships. This material would graphically illustrate the rich underwater cultural heritage which lies within the Sound. The area chosen for exploration lay in the north-west corner of the Sound between Wilderness Point to the north and the Bridge reef to the south. It was recorded that several ships had been wrecked there, so the team focussed their efforts on two in particular: the HMS *Harwich*, which sank off Wilderness Point and the fast French privateer brig *L'aimable Victoire*, which was wrecked on the Bridge reef.

Diving commenced off Wilderness Point in June 1973 in the deep-water channel which forms the entrance to the Hamoaze. The team began their search by exploring the sea-bed at the bottom of the channel's sheer western slope. They then progressed in a south-south-easterly direction. By early October they had reached the less severe north-west slope of the Bridge reef, which lay directly beneath the Raven's Cliffs of Mount Edgcumbe. So far their search had been fruitless. At Ravenness Point they swung around in a wide arc and began swimming towards Drake's Island.

Diorama of a late 18th century Danish shipyard.
By kind permission of the Flensburg Shipping Museum. Photo Ian Skelton.

TWO

Discovery

In late October, two members of the diving team, Colin Hannaford and Chris Holwill, were continuing the search at a depth of 30 metres. In the gloom their lamps cast ghostly beams of light across a flat mud seabed crawling with hundreds of black spidery starfish. On the surface, in a launch, the team leader watched intently as the diver's marker float slowly progressed towards Drake's Island. With just five minutes of their diving time left the float stopped moving and the two divers surfaced.

"Have you found anything?" shouted the boat crew hopefully.

Chris Holwill spat out his aqualung mouthpiece and pushed his face-mask onto his forehead. "Nothing very much" he replied, trying hard to suppress his excitement, "just an old ship's bell sticking out of the mud".

This was fantastic news. All the hours of searching had paid off. There was much excited speculation. Could there be a name on the bell? Was the ship it belonged to down there? If so, was it the warship HMS *Harwich* or the French privateer, *L'aimable Victoire?* Was it some other ship?

After the bell's position had been accurately marked on the seabed it was gently power-winched into the launch and placed in a holding tank. Then, when the dark grey silt was teased from its surface, everyone in the boat gasped. The beautifully decorated bronze bell was covered in writing. There was a date: 1782. There was detail of the vessel's sailing rig: Die (The) Brigantine. There was the name of the ship and its home port: *Die Frau Metta Catharina von Flensburg,* (The Mrs *Metta Catharina* from Flensburg). There was even the name of the bell founder: B. J. Beseler, from Rendsburg.

More divers descended to a probe, which marked the position where the bell had lain. They then scanned the sea floor. Three metres from the probe they saw a heavily encrusted iron anchor ring. Close by and extending northwards in orderly lines were bundles of leather, some of which were in surprisingly good condition. The team members now knew they had discovered a wrecked ship and not just a lone bronze bell. It was time to carry out some research.

A letter was sent to the Stadtisches Museum Flensburg, in the German state of Schleswig-Holstein. The Museum Director confirmed that the *Metta Catharina* was from Flensburg, having been built on the north shore of Flensburg Fiord in 1782. Her cargo capacity was 53 commercial lasts, (106 metric tonnes). Her owner and master between 1782 and 1787 were Hinrich Lorck of Flensburg and Knut Andersen. Her crew of six was captained by Hans Jensen Twedt, who was lost off Ireland in 1787.

The bronze bell from the *Metta Catharina* which led the divers to the wrecked ship and enabled them to identify it.

The diving team now knew the approximate year of the vessel's loss. Her owners no longer had possession after 1787, so this date was used as a reference point for further research. The following report was discovered:

The 10th inst: arrives the Christian from Rotterdam with wheat and cheese for Barcelona. In the night about 10 o'clock in a violent gale of wind from the south-west she drove on shore at Deadman's Bay in the Cattewater and it is to be much feared that the vessel and cargo will be lost. The crew all sound. Same night was drove on shore on Drake's Island the Metta Catharina of Flensburg bound from St Petersburg for Genoa laden with hemp and leather. Vessel and cargo entirely lost; crew saved (extract from a letter from Plymouth, 12 December, Sherborne Mercury 18 December 1786).

This contemporary newspaper report confirmed that the diving team had indeed discovered the wreck of the Flensburg brigantine *Metta Catharina* with her cargo of leather. The divers were relieved to find that none of the crew had gone down with the ship, but they had cause to wonder whether any remains of its structure had survived. Apart from the bell, the anchor and the bundles of leather, nothing could be seen protruding from the flat, featureless seabed. No masts, no bowsprit, no planking. If any ship's timbers did still exist, they would lay entombed deep beneath the sea floor. Burrowing downwards into the thick grey silt seemed a daunting prospect. But before reaching for their trowels and tape measures the team had to meet one very important obligation. As 'salvors in possession' they were duty-bound to find out who the present-day owner of the wrecked ship was.

Before the year 1864, Schleswig-Holstein was administered by Denmark and for that reason the team firstly approached the Danes. The Director of the Viking Ship Museum confirmed that the Danish state had no claim to the wreck. Because Germany annexed Schleswig-Holstein in 1864 the team next contacted the Director of the Altonaer Museum in Hamburg, who verified that they too had no claim to the ship, which, they pointed out had been lost in British territorial waters. Following these disclaimers from the Continent, a solicitor friend carried out research in the UK and determined that the Duchy of Cornwall had 'right of wreck' and was, therefore, the owner of the sunken *Metta Catharina* and her cargo. The Duke of Cornwall, His Royal Highness Prince Charles, who happens to be a diver himself and is President of the British Sub-Aqua Club, granted the team the right to survey and excavate the remains of the ship.

The team members were jubilant. They issued a press release and took part in radio and television interviews. Listeners and viewers were enthralled; stories of divers exploring sunken shipwrecks are always guaranteed to excite the public imagination.

THREE
Meeting the challenge

The discovery of the wreck of the *Metta Catharina* sparked a lively discussion at the next indoor meeting of the diving team. The name, which the team had given itself, was the Nautical Archaeology Section and they now had an archaeological project to cut their teeth on --- but what a formidable challenge it promised to be. The divers were under no illusions regarding the difficulties and dangers of working in such unfavourable environmental conditions. The remains of the ship were completely buried in dark grey, clay-like silt. The water over the site was twice as deep as the water in which Henry the 8th's *Mary Rose* lay. The seabed, which was swept by strong tides, was gloomy with little or no natural light. The underwater visibility was poor at the best of times, but sediments disturbed by working divers would often reduce this to stygian blackness.

The divers would also have to face the threat of physiological dangers when working at a depth of 30 metres. At that depth the high pressures, which their bodies are subjected to, forces nitrogen gas into their blood and tissues. If the diver then returns to the surface too rapidly this nitrogen will come out of solution and form gas bubbles within vital parts of the body. These bubbles will interfere with blood circulation causing rashes, joint-pain, numbness, breathing difficulties and even permanent disability or death. This disease is called decompression sickness or the 'bends'.

Two decompressing divers hold on to a rope below the diving boat, while the deadly nitrogen gases in their bodies are slowly released. This safety procedure reduces the risk of the 'bends'. *Photo. Ian Skelton.*

Another more insidious hazard is nitrogen narcosis, referred to by divers as 'rapture of the deeps'. This happens when the nitrogen gas under pressure in the diver's body causes an effect akin to drunkenness. The diver is often aware that this disease is affecting him, but it still results in poor judgement, impaired manual dexterity, extreme anxiety and in some instances, hallucinations and depression.

In addition to the environmental and physiological issues, there was a major practical problem which would need to be dealt with. Any fieldwork programme would need to be supported by adequate funding. The money would be required in order to provide a boat and a wide range of specialised materials and equipment. Various ways and means were suggested to generate funds. These included raffles, jumble sales, social events and scavenging the sea floor for scrap metal.

Faced with this formidable catalogue of difficulties a few team members questioned the feasibility of the project. However, after some debate, it was decided unanimously to shelve the search for HMS *Harwich* and *L'aimable Victoire* and to concentrate all efforts on the survey and excavation of the *Metta Catharina*.

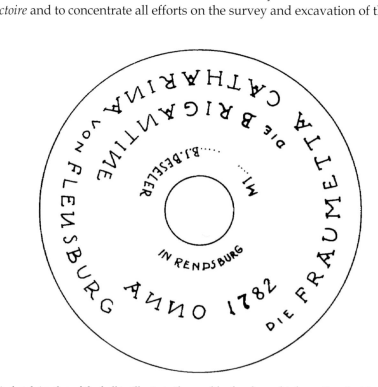

A sketch in plan of the bell to illustrate the wealth of embossed information, (not to scale).
Drawing. Wilf Jenkin.

FOUR

The Survey

Before any serious digging could be attempted on the sunken brigantine, the team were obliged, as responsible underwater archaeologists, to carry out a pre-disturbance survey of the entire wreck site. This involved marking out the four-hundred-square-metre area with a complex network of lines and triangulation stations. This arrangement helped the divers to orient themselves in the gloom whilst they sounded the whole area of seabed with steel probes. The probing work, spread over many months, provided a sub-bottom picture of the ship aligned longitudinally along a north/south axis. This alignment coincided with that of the exposed bundles of leather.

The next phase in the survey work involved taking samples from a selection of the contacts which had been struck by the steel probes. The samples were extracted by a long steel coring device which was pushed deep into the silt and then driven into the contact with a lump-hammer. This was exhausting work, but it produced the hoped-for "Eureka" moment when plugs of oak were successfully recovered from several positions. It was a time for celebration. The plugs of oak were proof that Captain Twedt's brigantine had survived two centuries of burial beneath the seabed of Plymouth Sound. The divers were elated, but how would they be able to uncover those ancient timbers so far below the sea floor?

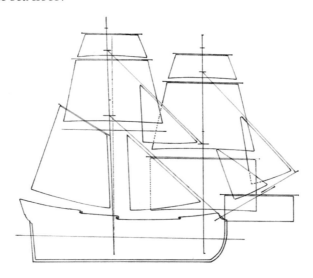

Sail plan of a late 18th century Danish brigantine.
Drawing by Ian Skelton from detail kindly supplied by the Danish Records Office.

FIVE
Early exploratory digging

The first attempt to uncover the oak timbers was with a water jet. A water pump was used to power a government-surplus fire-fighter's hose and nozzle. Sadly the jet was only successful in blasting the seabed sediments into dark billowing clouds. The clouds enveloped the jet operator, completely wiping out his visibility. The jet was soon abandoned in favour of a suction dredge. To form the dredge the hose and nozzle were connected to a long horizontal drainpipe. In operation water from the pump races through the pipe causing a gentle suction at the mouth-end. The suction picks up sediments and discharges them from the exhaust end of the pipe down-tide, well away from the operator. Although the dredge was an improvement on the water jet, it was too weak to make any worthwhile progress downwards into the sea floor.

The team now knew they needed a much more powerful tool. They realised that the only way they could reach the buried timbers was with the use of an airlift system. This realisation put them on the horns of a dilemma. Whereas the water pump and suction dredge were small, light and inexpensive, an airlift system would require very heavy and costly equipment, together with a large rigid boat --- it was not possible to operate airlifts from inflatable dive boats. The diving team was faced with a stark choice: 'bite the bullet' and find the means to acquire an airlift, or abandon the project altogether.

Winter diving. The dive boat *Catharina II* at anchor on the wreck site. *Photo. Ian Skelton.*

An airlift system, although bulky and expensive, is technically quite simple in principle. A heavy air compressor, of the type used to power pneumatic road drills, is bolted onto the deck of a boat. An airline is connected between the compressor and the lower end of an open-ended vertical tube, which is tethered to the seabed. When the diver-operator turns on a tap in the airline, the air from the compressor enters the bottom end of the tube and rushes upwards. This action creates suction at the bottom, (mouth-end), of the airlift tube. This powerful suction greedily gobbles up sediments, stones and shells from the sea floor and disgorges them from the open, (exhaust end), at the top of the tube where they are swept away by the strong tidal currents.

The decision to procure an airlift system was to have dire consequences for the diving team. With limited funds available a suitable boat could only be obtained by rebuilding a worn-out wooden hulk. A 36 year old government-surplus sailing cutter was purchased for £295 and aptly named *Catharina II*. Two years of hard work by eight dedicated members were needed to make the 32 ft boat seaworthy and capable of housing the 1.5 ton air compressor. The compressor had been generously donated by Comp-air Construction & Mining Limited, of Camborne in Cornwall. During those two years of toil the team membership shrank from 25 to eight. It was not all bad news, though. The Duchy of Cornwall kindly agreed that some of the leather could be sold to help fund the project. This freed the diminished team from other forms of fund-raising and allowed them more time to work on the boat and airlift.

Two divers use an airlift to remove the deep layer of silt which covers the *Metta Catharina*'s timbers.
Photo. Colin Hannaford

Members of the diving team proudly display a complete and well-preserved animal hide recovered from the shipwreck. From left to right: Team Leader and Author, Ian Skelton; Deputy Team Leader, Colin Hannaford; Team Engineer, Al Bunce. *Photo. Mike Evans.*

SIX
Opening the time capsule

During their first session on the wreck site, with the newly acquired boat and airlift system, the eight remaining members of the diving team were richly rewarded for their loyal commitment to the project. A small experimental airlift, just 4.5 metres long, was used to dig a pit at a position on the seabed where core-sampling had previously recovered plugs of oak. Sediments, which had been deposited over two centuries, were sucked into the hungry airlift's maw and disgorged from its exhaust into the speeding tide. Divers operating the airlift watched wide-eyed as coherent ship's timbers were rapidly exposed. First the hacked-off stump of the mainmast, then a pair of ship's pumps. These were followed by the pump-housing, a scatter of yellow hand-made firebricks from the hearth and a well-preserved bundle of leather.

The bundle of leather was recovered for analysis. The divers were amazed to discover that it contained six complete animal hides. At this point laboratory tests were carried out to ensure that the leather harboured no viable spores of anthrax bacteria. The bacterium, which can be fatal to humans, is known to survive in hostile environments for centuries. Happily all the tests proved negative. Samples of leather were then sent to a research laboratory and to the Museum of Leathercraft. By consensus, the hides from that bundle were identified as being most likely from reindeer. The leather, which was traditionally described as 'Russia Calf', had been treated by the age-old Russian method of tanning with willow bark and currying with birch oil.

More digging with the airlift near the mast uncovered several items from the galley, or cookhouse. In addition to the firebricks, which were chaotically scattered, there were remains of copper kettles, firewood for the hearth, butchered animal bones and Bellarmine flagons from the Rhineland. The flagons would have originally held olive oil and rum. Rum was a favoured drink of sailors and Flensburg is still known to this day for its rum. Its fame came in the mid 18th century when the sugar cane trade in Flensburg -- under Danish control at the time -- began trading with the Danish West Indies.

During the work near the mast a long probe was used to sound the pump well. The results confirmed that 80% of the pump-housing had survived. This exciting news satisfied the team that a large part of the *Metta Catharina* and her cargo lay buried under the sea floor. They were now aware they had opened a time capsule. With this in mind they decided to carry out a full-scale excavation of the ship abaft, (behind), the mainmast. This area would include the galley, the after cargo hold, the deckhouse and the stern. It was a thrilling prospect. They were set to journey back in time to the 18th century.

SEVEN
Sixteen fathoms beneath & counting

Excavating and surveying the remains of the wreck abaft the mainmast was much more demanding and time-consuming than was originally thought by even the most pessimistic member of the team. An original time estimate of five years would eventually stretch to 20 years. The level of difficulty was truly formidable. It has been argued that the wreck of the *Metta Catharina* represented the most difficult underwater archaeological project in the UK.

The problems encountered were myriad. The stiff bank of sediments, which covered the wreck, was four metres deep in places. This required the divers to create and work in pits nearly two fathoms below the sea floor. Sections from the sheer walls of the pits often broke away to form mud slides, which cascaded down onto the divers below. The visibility was frequently less than one metre, which meant the divers had to work in the darkness by feel alone. Gales regularly stripped hundreds of large kelp plants and other seaweeds from the shallows around the Bridge reef and dumped them on the wreck site filling the pits and trenches, which had been painstakingly excavated. Many bundles of leather were trapped beneath collapsed timbers, or were tightly jammed together. Removing the trapped bundles was energy-sapping and time-consuming. Other difficulties included equipment failure, bad weather, fouling of the site by fishing tackle and stray anchors, the narcotic effects of nitrogen gas, contrary tides, club politics and funding.

Many innovative ideas were conceived to overcome some of the more vexing problems. New airlifts were designed and built, each to carry out a specific task. The 'Beast' was constructed to suck away the stiff layers of deep sediment which entombed the ship. Underwater physics states that, the longer the airlift tube, the greater its power. The 15 centimetres diameter 'Beast' airlift tube was an eye-watering 14 metres long. The 'Beast' was aptly named. Its formidable power had the potential to cut into the thick banks of sediment like a hot knife into butter --- but divers beware --- this airlift could draw blood through a careless operator's skin, or snatch any dangling piece of kit with serious consequences. Another new airlift was the lusty 'Big Bertha'. Although 'Big Bertha' was only four metres long, it had a massive diameter of 27 centimetres and was fed by dual airlines. This airlift was designed to deal with the huge volumes of dead weed, which regularly invaded the work areas. 'Big Bertha' made short work of clearing these intrusive plants by gobbling them up in bundles and shooting them to the surface inside enormous bubbles of air. Other smaller airlifts were built to carry out the more delicate task of teasing shipboard artefacts from the silt.

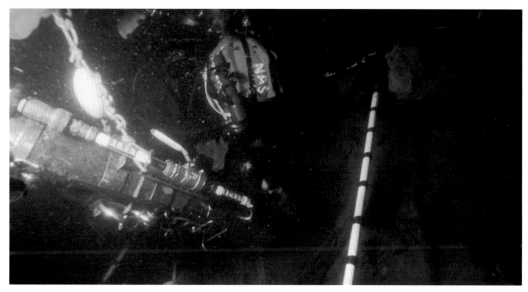

A diver uses the powerful fourteen-metres-long 'Beast' airlift to suck away sediments from above some of the *Metta Catharina's* cargo of leather. *Photo. Colin Hannaford.*

The weed-gobbling 'Big Bertha' airlift being retrieved by the safety boat at the end of a day's diving. *Photo. Ian Skelton.*

Bundles of 'Russia Calf' leather removed from the cargo hold and stacked ready to be raised to the surface.
Photo. Dan Burton.

Experimentation was often needed to provide a solution to a particular problem and as is so often the case with improvisation, unseen hazards will result. Trapped leather cargo frequently had to be removed in order to allow the excavation to proceed unhindered. Divers often had to grab a bundle of leather in a 'bear hug' and then, with both feet firmly planted in the silt, use the brute force of their legs to wrench it free. With concerns for diver's safety, a novel method of pulling out the trapped leather was called for. The first experiment involved the hammering of a 30 centimetre-long steel spike into the end of a bundle and then connecting the spike to a large bag filled with air. This proved to be a dangerous operation as the author, Ian Skelton, discovered to his cost. He suffered a narrow escape when the spike unexpectedly broke free and shot violently upwards, trapping his lifeline and dragging him rapidly towards the surface. Eventually the basic idea was refined and rendered safe to use. In place of the steel spike, a large modified G-cramp was employed to grip the bundle and a smaller less buoyant air bag was used to exert the pull.

EIGHT
Chaos in the stern

With many technical problems overcome and with huge volumes of thick sediment removed from the wreck abaft the mainmast by the 'Beast' airlift, digging in the stern section proceeded apace. The results of the digging were disappointing and puzzling in equal measure. There was no rudder, no transom, no planking and amazingly no keel. There was no coherent ship's structure at all. Many large timber beams were uncovered, but all had been severely damaged by hungry wood-boring marine creatures including the dreaded 'shipworm'. Spilled strips and bundles of decaying leather lay mixed with pulley-blocks from the ship's rigging, pottery, glassware, tobacco pipes and rotting fragments of decking. Years of delicate excavation work were needed to pick through this chaotic jumble.

On the port side of the stern section, close to the after cargo hold, a large concentration of shipboard items was recovered from a small area. This material included tunic buttons, shoe buckles, navigational instruments, wine and spirits bottles, musket balls and a human leg bone. Two interpretations were put forward for this eclectic mix. One suggestion proposed that strong tidal currents scoured a deep pit in the seabed into which the deckhouse and its contents eventually collapsed. A second theory held that immediately after the storm in 1786, local boatmen attempted to salvage material from the sunken wreck by grappling and in doing so, broke up the deckhouse and dragged its remains across the deck to the port side. Whichever interpretation was correct, the divers were once again faced with the intricate task of teasing scores of shipboard items from a tangled web of decomposing leather and worm-riddled wood. This task was carried out at the bottom of a deep dark pit with little or no visibility. The work called for experienced, level-headed divers of exceptional ability.

One final task carried out in the stern area was a daring attempt to locate the *Metta Catharina's* keel. A group of three heavy 'V' – shaped oak timbers stood in a row between the stern area and the after cargo hold. It had been previously noted that all three of these timbers had been violently split into two during the wrecking event. The timbers, called floors, should have been connected to the keel. A plan was hatched to tunnel beneath them to look for the missing keel timber. Months were spent digging through stiff, clay-like silt until a diver was able to wriggle down into the tunnel below the floors. Despite searching with a powerful lantern and probing with a long pointed steel rod he was unable to locate any trace of the keel.

A group of items from the *Metta Catharina's* rigging. The pulley-wheels, called sheaves, are of *Lignum vitae*. The pulley block is similar to blocks used today. *Photo. Ian Skelton.*

Two questions dogged the team members after completing their work in the stern. Why were there human remains in the wreck and why was there no sign of the keel? The divers could only speculate on the first question: either contemporary newspaper reports had been wrong and a crew member had gone down with the ship, or some poor unfortunate had drowned in Plymouth Sound shortly after the sinking and his body had been washed into the sunken *Metta Catharina* by the fierce tidal currents. The divers were more bullish about the second question, though. They were convinced that some of the keel must have survived, because the mainmast was still standing upright. They reasoned that the mast would still be connected to the keelson, which in turn would be bolted to the keel, therefore there should be at least some remnants of the keel timber close behind the mast in the after cargo hold.

Before the divers were able to test this theory, though, a major logistical problem reared its ugly head: their beloved diving boat, the *Catharina II,* was declared no longer fit for purpose by a marine surveyor. Once again the dedicated few in the diving team found themselves in a quandary. How difficult would it be to acquire a replacement boat and what effect would the effort involved have on the *esprit de corps?*

NINE
The Catharina III

After much discussion and after three senior members of the diving team had researched all the options, it was decided unanimously to build a brand new, 'no frills' dive boat from a basic kit. The boat chosen was the 'Offshore 105', a 10 metres long GRP fast fishing boat designed by Rod Baker of Port Isaac Workboats, Wadebridge, Cornwall. Sadly, once again some of the divers in the team dropped out, leaving just seven dedicated members to carry out the building work. Fortunately the seven were willing to give up all diving activity during the build period and as a result the *Catharina III* was constructed from scratch in just eight months. The shiny new boat was fitted with an air compressor to power the airlifts and a davit and cradle to house the inflatable safety tender. Although everyone in the team was sad to say goodbye to the faithful old *Catharina II,* they all acknowledged that the new replacement was roomier, more stable and a safer platform to dive from.

The new dive boat, the *Catharina III*, anchored on the dive site below the Raven's Cliffs of Mount Edgcumbe. The yellow cowl of the air compressor can be seen in the stern. The appropriate diving signals are displayed on the mast. *Photo. Ian Skelton.*

Eclectic mix of bottles sourced from northern Europe. All were hand-blown and all show the flaws and lack of symmetry associated with this method of manufacture. *Photo. Ian Skelton.*

Tunic buttons of brass, bone and pewter. The pewter button with the fouled anchor design is similar to those worn by marine officers during the 18th century. *Photo. Ian Skelton.*

An ornately decorated brass tobacco box. The initials D K are believed to be the owner's initials. Engraved symbols include a staved cask, an orb, an hour glass with wings to signify *Tempus fugit*, (time flies) and a ladder.
Photo. Ian Skelton

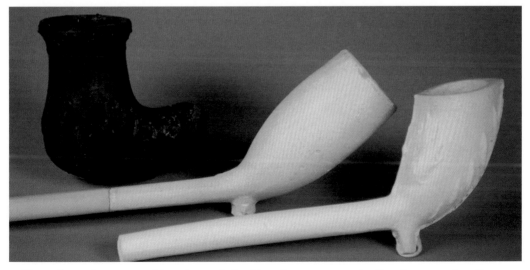

Three tobacco pipes recovered from the wreck. Smoking tobacco was a popular diversion among the sailors on board the *Metta Catharina* despite the risk of fire aboard a ship composed of wood, canvas and tar. *Photo. Ian Skelton.*

TEN
Cargo hold, 'common pumps' & keel

The after cargo hold of the *Metta Catharina* extended a distance of 5.5 metres north, (aft), from the mainmast. During earlier excavation work it was discovered that this hold was jam-packed with bundles of animal hides, many of which were still lashed together with lengths of dried grass. To fully explore the hold all of this cargo had to be removed. The removal work uncovered more shipboard items including wine and spirits bottles, pottery, Russian lead customs seals, pulley-blocks and parts of a flintlock pistol. With the cargo removed the floor of the hold was revealed. The floor's centre section was filled with heavy ballast stones. These rough stones were covered with a carpet of woven grass matting to protect the hides. All of this ballast had to be painstakingly put into bins and dragged off the site.

The exposed timbers in the after cargo hold after removal of cargo, ballast stones and some of the planking. The large central timber is the keelson. Curved ribs, (or frames), lie beneath the keelson and ceiling planks occupy the top right-hand corner of the photo. The brightly coloured tube is the airlift nozzle. *Photo. Colin Hannaford.*

When the floor was cleared and swept clean by the airlifts the divers were thrilled to discover that all the timber structure, which had been protected by the cargo and ballast, was in an excellent state of preservation. The sight was truly awesome. The base of the mainmast, planed to the conventional octagonal shape, was firmly slotted into its step in the keelson and was held there by a carved oak chock. The two ship's pumps stood bolt upright from their seatings in the well and the thick oak floor planks --- which sailors paradoxically refer to as ceilings --- were still held firmly in position by large wood dowels. These 30 millimetre dowels are called treenails; pronounced by shipwrights as 'trunnels'. Sections of outer hull planking could also be seen. These sturdy oak timbers were 60 millimetres thick. They were covered with a sacrificial layer of thin pine fastened with iron nails. Sandwiched between the oak and the pine planking was a layer of pitch and horsehair. The shipwrights, who built the *Metta Catharina*, believed this layer would deter the dreaded 'shipworm'. They were wrong.

The exposed mainmast base is shown in the centre of the photo with the starboard pump tube to the right, (the port pump has been removed). The carved oak chock in the foreground holds the mast securely within its step in the keelson. *Photo. Colin Hannaford.*

With the cargo no longer in position to support the mainmast and pumps, the relentless tidal currents which swept across the seabed , threatened to push them down onto the divers below. To forestall this hazard it was decided to raise them for recording and analysis. When the mast was lifted from the keelson it was noted that no 'lucky' coin lay within the mast-step. Those with a superstitious turn of mind will not be surprised to hear of that discovery.

Discoveries of greater consequence were made when the ship's pumps were examined on dry land. They were identified as 'common pumps' and had been made from sections of pine tree, which had been drilled through to create tubes. No remains of pump handles were attached. Were the handles ripped from their seatings by wreckers with heavy iron grapnels shortly after the *Metta Catharina* had sunk? Or had they been removed by the crew?

Even more surprisingly, a water-level measuring rod, made of oak, was found inside the starboard pump tube. To make room for this rod all the workings of that pump would have been removed. That action would have rendered the pump useless. The implication of this startling evidence is that the Captain, concerned to keep his valuable cargo dry, had decided it was more important to keep a tight check on the level of the bilge-water than to have both his pumps in working order. Was that a calamitous mistake?

With the floor of the cargo hold made safe the divers were able to carry on their search for the missing keel. Once again the work was arduous and time-consuming. Several planks on the floor of the hold were removed to allow digging to take place in the void beneath. Because the gaps in the exposed structure within the void were narrow, a small-diameter nozzle had to be fitted to one of the airlifts. The diver/excavator had to lie face down in order to break up the well-compacted silt in the void with a long-handled trowel.

After weeks of digging the intact top of the keel was uncovered less than an arms-length from the mainmast step. The digging then continued further back into the hold until a break in the keel was found at a distance of just two metres from the mainmast step. This discovery was both exciting and sobering. It was exciting, because a mystery which had puzzled the team members for so long had been solved after much hard work. It was sobering, because it provided clear evidence of the nightmarish conditions suffered by Hans Twedt and his crew on that fateful night in December 1786. The interpretation was stark. Punished by sledge-hammer blows as the stricken *Metta Catharina* plunged through the breakers across the Bridge reef, the huge keel timber had finally snapped like a rotten tooth. That would have been the instant when the frantic clamouring of the ship's bell segued to a mournful death knell. The brigantine and her cargo were doomed.

ELEVEN
Braving the bow

Excavating in the bow area tested the stamina and resourcefulness of the diving team to the absolute limit. As a first measure all the heavy airlift mooring sinkers and the huge dive-boat mooring anchor had to be moved to the forward section of the wrecked ship. The second phase of this tortuous logistical operation was the fixing of extra triangulation stations to aid survey work, together with the laying of high-visibility guidelines to orient the divers.

The plan for work in the bow area was to first locate the foremast. If the mast could be found it would lead to the uncovering of the forecastle and bow structure. In practice, digging in the bow area was more difficult than in the after cargo hold and stern areas. The upper layer of loose sediment was packed with stones, slates and scallop shells. Some of the stones were 15 centimetres across. Despite the use of filter attachments, airlift blockages were frequent. Items too large to pass through the filters were dropped into bins and dragged off the site.

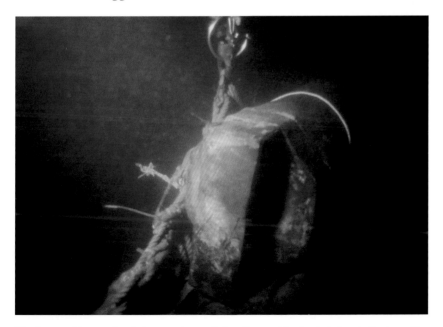

The foremast is one of only two masts on a brigantine and is situated close to the bow. The photo shows the base of the *Metta Catharina's* foremast, planed to the conventional octagonal shape and cut to form a tenon which slotted into the mast step. *Photo. Colin Hannaford.*

As the digging progressed in the bow area, bundles of leather were soon uncovered lying together just below the sea floor. Within the uppermost layers the leather was so decayed it resembled wet cardboard. All material in this condition was taken off site. As the digging moved downwards the condition of the hides improved, but their removal became progressively more difficult. The bundles were all tightly jammed together and several were interlocked. Many of these trapped bundles were extracted by force with G-cramps and air bags. At this point the diving team, whose numbers had declined, were joined by divers from Plymouth University. The university divers were well-trained and bursting with energy and enthusiasm. During the last year of work on the wreck site they were a huge asset.

Over many months, as the excavation progressed forward to the south, a large semicircular pit was created. As the pit deepened the difficulties increased. The fierce currents set up vortices within the pit reducing visibility to zero. The currents also washed large quantities of debris from the unstable rim of the pit down into the work area. Additionally, much of the grass matting around the leather had become brittle and when disturbed, disintegrated into clouds of swirling chaff. A further problem occurred in the autumn when huge volumes of dead seaweed were swept into the pit by the tides. Added to these hindrances was the effort needed to stow the airlifts at the end of each day's diving. As the pit walls became higher and steeper the task of hauling these heavy tools back up to the sea floor became ever more challenging.

Despite these setbacks the foremast was eventually discovered. Its jagged top was revealed just below seabed level close to its predicted position. When the press of cargo supporting it was removed, the force of the tidal currents pushed it from its step. Once again no 'lucky' coin was found in the step. Further digging to each side of the mast-step revealed no substantial timber structure. On both sides of the bow area spilled bundles of leather were found outside the predicted limits of the ship's hull. Spilled bundles were also found immediately south of the foremast's position. A few shipboard items were recovered from the area, including a Russian lead cargo seal, a large pulley-block, fragments of leather footwear and an iron cannonball.

Sadly, at this time, it became necessary to terminate all fieldwork on the site. After 32 years of service the team leader wished to retire and with no-one able to pick up the reins, the decision was made to wind up the venture. A final clear-up operation was carried out on the site, which involved returning the masts and any loose cargo to the pit floor and the removal of fixtures. As far as was practicable the site was restored to its original condition. A site survey carried out a year later by the Plymouth University divers confirmed that silting had completely buried all the previously-exposed remains of the brigantine. The *Metta Catharina* would, from now on, be left to rest in peace.

TWELVE
Picking up the pieces

The *Metta Catharina* is not a ship of exceptional historical significance, such as the *Vasa* or the *Mary Rose*. Nor is it a treasure ship such as the HMS *Association* or the *Hollandia*. Its archaeological merit lies in the fact that it is a fine example of the many hundreds of small 18th century Baltic traders which plied the European shipping routes. The chance find by the Plymouth diving team offered a unique opportunity to open a time capsule, which had lain entombed in the seabed of Plymouth Sound since December 1786. By the systematic excavation and survey of the wrecked ship the diving team was able to study one of the less well-documented Baltic merchantmen, her remarkable cargo and details surrounding the circumstances of her loss.

A selection of pottery recovered from the wreck. From left to right: a stoneware flagon from Belgium; a Flemish salt-glazed cruet; a silver-grey stoneware flagon from the German Rhineland; a stoneware jar from France and a large stoneware flagon from the German Rhineland. *Photo. Ian Skelton.*

Brass shoe buckle with toothed loop & two-tined fork. *Ian Skelton*

The excavation of any shipwreck is by its very nature destructive and must, therefore, be carried out with great care in order not to damage any important material, or lose any significant information. It cannot be overemphasised that the remains of any vessel being picked over by archaeologists represents a part of some country's maritime heritage. With this in mind the Plymouth divers carefully plotted the position of every item they recovered. They knew that the precise location of the items and their relationship to each other can often tell as much about the ship and her crew as the articles themselves.

Once out of the sea-water each item had to be carefully treated to prevent its disintegration. The bronze bell was chemically stabilised by a conservator at Bristol Museum. Since then the team members have managed to conserve most of the items themselves. After conservation each article has been drawn and photographed to a high standard. This is archaeology and far removed from the 'plundering' of shipwreck sites which often took place in the past.

On the seabed the diver's work, although hazardous, offers frequent rewards as he picks up the pieces left behind from a way of life long past. The thrill of teasing a well-smoked tobacco pipe, or a fancy shoe-buckle from its ancient bed of silt, or handling a Bellarmine flagon, which once carried sailor's rum from Denmark is deeply evocative. The all-pervading gloom of the sea floor and the monotonous hiss and bubble of the aqualung can be forgotten for a while as the diver calls to mind images of Danish seamen with rings in their ears and whiskers curled in ringlets and tarry pigtails and their swaggering clumsy sea-walk as they stomped around the pitching deck of the *Metta Catharina*. For many of the divers in the team, the prospect of experiencing these tantalising glimpses into the lives of ordinary 18th century mariners is what spurred them to venture down into the wrecked ship year after year.

Door lock. Probably from the Captain's quarters. *Ian Skelton*

On one occasion, though, a diver's discovery quickly turned into a bad dream. He returned to the surface beaming with delight after forty minutes of digging. In the boat he proudly presented the team leader with the results of his efforts: a 'Delftware bowl' filled with grey silt. But alas, his smile soon faded when he was told that his treasured bowl was in fact the upper section of a human skull. He later confessed that he didn't sleep well that night.

During 32 years of diving work on the wreck an eclectic mix of items were recovered. Putting these pieces together formed a fascinating picture of life aboard the ship. The number of bottles suggested that the mind-numbing routine and discomfort of life at sea was eased with alcohol. The collection of pipes and a tobacco-box indicated that smoking was tolerated despite the risk of fire aboard a ship composed of wood, canvas and tar. All the pottery was flawed seconds, which suggested that breakages were frequent in rough seas.

Weapons were carried aboard the *Metta Catharina*. This was a sensible precaution when venturing into the pirate-infested Mediterranean of the 18th century. The remains of a flintlock pistol were discovered. Also found were brass trigger-guards; lead musket and pistol shot; lead blunderbuss shot and an iron cannonball from a swivel gun.

The Captain's wine glass.
Ian Skelton

Many personal items were recovered from what was believed to be a collapsed deckhouse. This suggested that the deckhouse was used as living quarters in order to free up space below decks for extra cargo --- cramming the ship with as much cargo as possible optimised profits for the owners. The personal items included a variety of shoe-buckles made from brass and pewter; tunic buttons of bone, brass and pewter; leather footwear; a brass 'chamber' candle-stick complete with candle; a lead token embossed with a unicorn and dated 1785; a brass lock in three pieces; a bone tunic brush and a red dyewood sail-maker's marlin spike, or fid. Of special interest was a bone and wax bottle-stopper. The wax carried a positive imprint of Captain Hans Jensen Twedt's signet ring. The imprint was a heart crowned with a ship and divided into three sections by strands of rope and a flower. Each of the three sections contained one of the Captain's initials: H. J and T. The heart was supported on both its sides by fish (*hauriant*).

Scattered among the personal belongings were several pieces of navigational equipment. There were two heavy sounding leads. These were used to measure the depth of water beneath the ship's hull. There was a wood backstaff --- the forerunner of the modern-day sextant. Also recovered were an object-lens and two eyepieces from a telescope; a pair of brass compasses; a pair of brass dividers and a pair of brass sights from the ship's azimuth steering compass. Another item recovered, which would have been used in conjunction with a log-line to measure the brigantine's speed, was half of a sandglass. This globular ampoule of thin translucent glass miraculously survived the wrecking event. Its successful recovery bears testament to the skill and patience of the diver, who painstakingly coaxed it from its bed of silt at the bottom of a deep dark pit. All of these pieces of navigational equipment combine to offer an insight into the nautical skills which were needed to keep the *Metta Catharina* at sea.

A large serving plate decorated with the painting of a lady.
Ian Skelton

Other items of glassware, which were skilfully recovered from the silt, included three small medicine bottles of thinly blown glass and a wine glass with baluster stem and basal knop. As was the case with all bottles from the wreck, the contents of the medicine bottles had long ago been replaced by sea-water under pressure. The bottles do indicate, though, that curatives were carried on board. The wine glass was a high-status item and would have belonged to the Captain, who was probably the only aesthete on the ship.

In addition to the bronze bell other ship's fittings recovered included a total of 66 pulley-wheels from the rigging. These wheels, referred to by sailors as sheaves, or 'shivs', were all turned from a dense tropical hardwood known as *Lignum vitae*, (Latin for wood of life), and were too tough for marine wood-borers to eat, hence their survival. Many had suffered heavy use, which presented as chipping around the grooves and elongation of the axle, (or pin), holes. Two were fitted with cast-bronze bearings. These two would have been fitted into the elm pulley-blocks which hoisted and lowered the heavy sails. Only two complete, well-preserved pulley-blocks were found. These had been protected from attack by marine wood-boring creatures by spilled bundles of leather cargo. Also recovered were a brass cabin door lock and a small section of the brigantine's copper nameplate. The nameplate, which was decorated with elaborate scrollwork, would have adorned the stern.

From the beginning the divers realised that, due to time and funding constraints, they would be unable to uncover and explore all of the *Metta Catharina's* remains. It was considered sensible, therefore, to concentrate efforts on the stern; the accommodation area; one cargo hold and part of the bow. Perhaps for this reason no remains of the cargo of hemp were discovered. Although less inspiring than the 'Russia Calf' leather, hemp was the raw material of rope-making and arguably more important than leather in the days of sail.

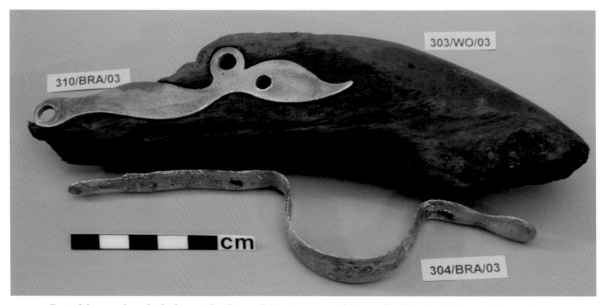

Part of the wood stock, the brass side-plate and the trigger-guard from a flintlock pistol. None of the steel components survived long-term immersion in sea-water. *Photo. Ian Skelton*

Part of a wood backstaff. This important navigational device was the forerunner of the sextant. It is sometimes referred to as the Davis Quadrant after its inventor Captain John Davis. It was used to measure the angle of the sun over the horizon. *Photo. Ian Skelton.*

This ampoule of thin translucent glass was one half of a sandglass, used to measure the speed of the ship. The complete sandglass would have been housed in a wood frame.
Photo. Ian Skelton.

Parts of a small hand telescope. From left to right: a bell-shaped eyepiece cover; the object lens - 64 mm in diameter; another eyepiece cover.
Photo. Ian Skelton.

THIRTEEN
Tsarist leather

Ever since the wreck of the *Metta Catharina* was discovered, her cargo of 'Russia Calf' leather has fascinated the diving community and the public at large. The leather, which was particularly water resistant, was *en route* to Genoa in the Mediterranean, a city famed for the manufacture of fine boots for gentlefolk. When violent weather intervened to hurl vessel and cargo into the depths of Plymouth Sound, the timbers of the ship and the bundles of leather should have been condemned to complete annihilation. Four factors combined to prevent this happening. Firstly, the ship settled into a bed of silt, which was later added to when silt levels in the Sound increased, following the building of the breakwater. The freshly deposited silt covered the wreck to create a stable, oxygen-free environment, which slowed decomposition. Secondly, the age-old Russian method of tanning the leather with willow bark and currying it with birch oil had rendered it water resistant. Thirdly, Hans Twedt, keen to completely fill the ship for maximum profit, had ordered the bundles of hides to be jammed into the holds as tightly as possible. This action helped preserve the hides and the timbers against which they pressed. Fourthly, at 30 metres depth, there is no wave action to pummel and pound any exposed material.

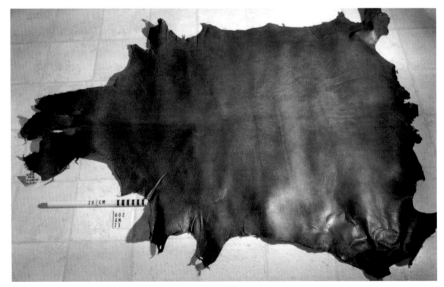

A complete animal hide from Tsarist Russia, photographed after receiving expert conservation treatment by skilled Cornish craftsman, Robin Snelson. *Photo. Ian Skelton.*

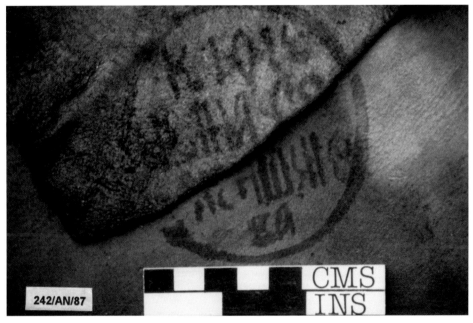

Many of the bundles of hides were stamped on their flesh sides. The lettering within the stamps was in the Cyrillic alphabet and represented the abbreviated names of the Russian exporting companies. *Photo. Ian Skelton.*

Almost all the bundles of leather were composed of six complete animal hides. The hides, which came from a variety of different animals, were tightly rolled together and bound with lengths of dried grass. They ranged in size from 1.65 x 0.8 metres to 2.1 x 1.3 metres. Many were complete with tail and a few still retained small patches of hair. The culling method which resulted in these size variations is not fully understood. It's possible that entire herds were slaughtered, or the hides could have been sourced from many different parts of Russia. Further research into the 18th century leather trade may one day provide an answer to this question.

The colours of the hides varied between dark coffee brown, chestnut and bright orange. Some were dappled with dark patches caused by contamination from seabed sediments. All the hides had a pleasing musky scent, which was a by-product of the Russian bark-tanning process. All were decorated on the finished side with a criss-cross pattern, which had been embossed by a heavy steel cylinder cut with many small ridges close together. All carried knife marks on their flesh sides. Many were marked with letters of the Cyrillic, (Russian) alphabet. Flesh-side markings were applied by ink stamp and finished-side markings were incised with a blade. The markings represented the abbreviated names of the Russian exporters.

Lead cargo seal bearing the Russian Imperial coat-of-arms; the name Port St Petersburg written in Cyrillic and the date 1786. The barrel emblem may represent customs, but this is uncertain. *Photo. Ian Skelton.*

Discovered alongside some of the cargo were lead seals issued by the Russian Customs authorities and by the Russian Quality Control Inspectorate. The seals issued by customs carried the crowned double-headed eagle of Imperial Russia with orb and sceptre, whilst those issued by quality control were stamped with initials and dates.

As well as raising funds for the diving project, some leather had other valuable uses. Hides were donated to the Mary Rose Trust and Parks Canada to help their scientists carry out research on the treatment of ancient leather from submerged sites. In 1986 the 200th anniversary of the loss of the *Metta Catharina* prompted Filofax to produce a limited version of their personal organisers from the leather. A £3,250 share of the sales went to the RNLI. London shoemakers, New & Lingwood, made 11 pairs of shoes from the leather. One pair was presented to Prince Charles, whilst a raffle was held for the privilege of purchasing the remainder at £1,250 per pair. Names of the buyers-to-be were drawn by the headmaster of Eton public school. Proceeds of the sale were donated to a hospice chosen by Prince Charles.

In the grey early morning light of December 11th 1786, as Hans Twedt gazed sadly out at the scatter of flotsam, which pitched and rolled in the swells close to Mount Edgcumbe, he could not have imagined that one day some of his precious cargo of 'Russia Calf' leather would return from the deep to be fashioned into fine footwear fit for a future King.

FOURTEEN
Mishaps aplenty

"There will always be those divers who get sufficient satisfaction from the act of diving itself to keep them contented. Many more, however, will want to occupy their time underwater more profitably once the skills of diving have been mastered." This second sentence from a statement made by the renowned nautical archaeologist, Joan du Plat Taylor, who died in 1983 at the age of 77, aptly described many of the 220 divers who enthusiastically applied their underwater skills on the wreck of the *Metta Catharina*. The divers, who wished to join the project, came from all over the UK; from the armed forces; the police; from universities and even from diving clubs as far afield as Austria and Canada. Those divers, although carrying bulky life support systems and working in an environment more hostile than the surface of the moon, proved themselves able to perform a range of difficult and complex underwater tasks. However, despite painstaking efforts to promote safe diving practices, with more than 4,500 man-hours spent underwater, there were bound to be mishaps from time to time.

A few divers suffered from decompression sickness --- 'the bends' --- even though they obeyed all the rules to the letter. The rules, or decompression tables, as they are referred to are not infallible. Some divers were just unlucky. Two divers suffered 'spinal bends' through no fault of their own. Happily, after expert treatment in the recompression chamber at the Diving Diseases Research Centre in Plymouth, they recovered without permanent injury. During the latter years of the project, the risk of the 'bends' was reduced by new technology. All divers then carried computers, which automatically calculated their depths; times; ascent rates and decompression procedures. Decompression 'stops' were carried out whilst clinging to a weighted line suspended beneath the boat. The 'stop' periods, usually 30 minutes or more, allowed the deadly nitrogen gas to seep from the diver's body slowly, rather than fizzing out like a freshly opened bottle of pop.

Another technical innovation was the use of oxygen enriched air, known as nitrox. The percentage of oxygen gas in the diver's aqualung was increased, thus reducing the percentage of the troublesome nitrogen gas. Nitrox allowed the diver to spend more time on the seabed, whilst also reducing the risk of contracting the 'bends'. As a bonus the smaller amount of nitrogen gas also reduced the risk of nitrogen narcosis --- the 'rapture of the deeps'.

Other serious incidents occurred, but fortunately without injury. One of these happened when three divers were working with the 'Beast' airlift. Close to the end of their dive time, with air cylinders nearly empty, they prepared to ascend. At this point, a vital air-hose on one diver's aqualung exploded, pouring his last reserves of air into the sea. With 30 metres of water above his head he was left with no life support system. He signalled to diver two that he needed to share his air --- correct procedure in this life-or-death situation. Air sharing began, but diver two became entangled with the airlift and stopped sharing. Diver one then began sharing with diver three. No one was able to recall what happened next, but for some reason diver one and diver three became separated. Diver one's situation was now desperate. He had no air and no companions. Only his 18 years of diving experience and excellent physical fitness saved him from drowning. With the air in his lifejacket providing buoyancy, he swam rapidly to the surface alone. He risked bursting his lungs; the 'bends' and black-out, but there was no other option. Luckily he made it with no ill effects. As a result of this life-threatening incident, divers were each equipped with an additional, separate breathing set for use in an emergency.

Another serious threat to the divers came from hazardous debris, which was sometimes pushed into the pits and trenches by the fierce currents. Stray fishing nets posed the greatest threat due to the risk of entanglement with the diver and his equipment. On one occasion a diver, who had been working alone whilst connected to the boat by a lifeline, returned to the surface and warned everyone that there was a large fishing net spread out on the sea floor close to the edge of the pit. A pair of divers then descended with a plan for removing the hazard. On the seabed there was no sign of the net. Exchanging shrugs the two divers sank down to the pit floor where the visibility was zero. After working only by feel for 15 minutes in stygian blackness, diver one pressed an object into diver two's hand. Diver two was thrilled. The object was small, polished and cylindrical in shape. It felt just like the French butter jar that had been found a few weeks earlier. Then, as he felt further, he found it was connected to a tangle of monofilament line. At that point he was gripped by an icy chill. The object in his hand was not an item of 18th century tableware --- it was a modern-day fishing net float. He and his companion were lying in complete darkness on the floor of a deep pit in company with a large fishing net. They had swum into a death trap. Years of experience held panic at bay. With each keeping a cool head they inched their way backwards out of the pit without entanglement. The net was then pulled from the pit by carefully positioned air bags and sent to the surface for safe disposal.

Some accidents were caused by the divers themselves, due to complacency. A recurring problem was the failure to tether a working airlift. An airlift tube, when propelling a mixture of rising bubbles and sediment up through its length, is safe to use. But if its bottom, (mouth-end), suffers a blockage, its entire length is instantly filled with air and becomes dangerously buoyant: the 'Beast', for example, would attain an upward thrust of 180 kilograms, (3.5 hundredweights). Fortunately most incidents involving un-tethered blocked airlifts only resulted in a red face and a scare for the diver concerned.

One such incident, though, was truly horrific and could have caused serious injury to the two divers concerned. Diver one was tasked to operate the formidable 14-metres-long 'Beast. He wasn't aware that the diver, who had used the airlift before him had, for some unknown reason, severed the upper safety tether. To compound the situation, diver one failed to connect the lower safety tether --- an accident was now waiting to happen.

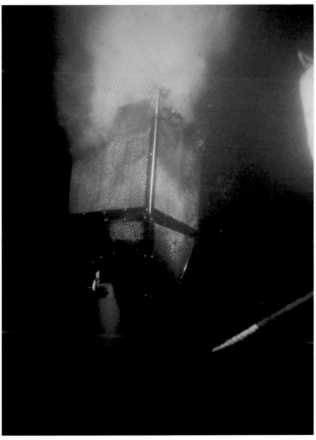

A strainer attachment was often fitted to the airlift's top end to catch any tiny items, such as tunic buttons, which may have otherwise been lost. The rope on the right-hand side of the photo is the airlift's upper safety tether. *Photo. Colin Hannaford.*

A diver uncovers a barnacle-encrusted Dutch 'onion' bottle from the grey silt
with the use of an airlift. *Photo. Paul Dart.*

Shortly after diver one began operating the 'Beast' its powerful suction snatched the front of his
lifejacket and dragged it into its maw. This caused an immediate blockage. Diver one was now
helplessly pinioned and with arms flailing, he was violently pulled off the seabed. Luckily, diver
two, who had been carrying out survey work close by, saw what was happening. He rushed to the
rescue and grabbed the airlift and diver one. As the 'Beast' shot towards the surface, diver two tried
desperately to reduce its air supply, whilst also attempting to free the trapped lifejacket. With ears
popping from the rapid pressure change the two divers hit the surface. Team members in the boat
described the unexpected emergence of the 'Beast' from the depths as resembling a 'Polaris' missile
launch. During the do-or-die struggle which followed, diver two managed to drag the lifejacket from
the airlift's mouth. Then, by controlling its air intake, he adjusted the airlift's buoyancy until he was
able to guide it back down to the seabed. Diver one followed alongside, shaken but unscathed. The
incident was a grim reminder to all concerned that airlifts are powerful tools and must be treated with
great respect.

Despite the hazardous nature of nautical archaeology, for more than 32 years the core members of the
diving team maintained a robust commitment towards piecing together the fascinating story of the
Metta Catharina and her amazing cargo; a story which has never failed to capture the attention of a
world-wide audience.

FIFTEEN
Telling the story

From the very beginning, when the media reported that a beautifully decorated bronze bell had been recovered by divers from a shipwreck in Plymouth Sound, the general public were captivated. As time passed and the story of a lost Danish brigantine and her cargo of Russian leather gradually unfolded, members of the diving team took every opportunity to engage with the community at large. Newspaper and magazine articles were published. Radio and television features were broadcast. Talks were given to a wide range of associations --- from schools to scout troops; from diner's clubs to diving clubs and from Rotary Clubs to wreck conferences.

In 1984 Flensburg celebrated its 700th anniversary. To mark the occasion the town hosted a gathering of 'tall ships' from the Sail Training Association. They also opened their brand new Shipping Museum. They invited the Leader of the Plymouth diving team, Ian Skelton and the Deputy Leader, Colin Hannaford, to attend the celebrations and to bring with them the bell from the *Metta Catharina*. Amid much pomp and ceremony Ian and Colin sailed into Flensburg Fiord with the bell aboard the sail training ship *Sir Winston Churchill*. The throng of Flensburg folk on the quayside cheered with delight as the Plymouth divers presented the bell to Frau Ingrid Gross, the town President.

For Ian and Colin the experience brought the whole story of the bell into sharp focus --- from its cheerful clamouring during the launching ceremony in 1782; to its task of heralding the 'dog watches' throughout four years at sea; to its mournful tolling during the fateful night of the wrecking; to its 200 years of slumber at the bottom of Plymouth Sound and finally to its return to its home port in Flensburg Fiord.

Although the bronze bell from the *Metta Catharina* is considered iconic, many other shipboard items have been recovered from the wreck for display to the general public. Several large-scale exhibitions have been held in the UK allowing interested audiences to learn more about life at sea in the 18th century. Visitors to the displays have seen hand-blown wine and spirits bottles sourced from all over northern Europe; stoneware jars and flagons from the Rhineland; a selection of tobacco pipes together with an elaborately decorated tobacco box; buckles of pewter and brass; tunic buttons of pewter, brass and bone; telescope components; sounding leads and cargo seals issued by the Russian Customs.

A few years after the bell had been returned to the people of Flensburg, the entire collection of shipboard items from the wreck were transported to their world-class Shipping Museum for a major display. Flensburg folk are extremely proud of their maritime heritage and were delighted to view the exhibition of material from their long lost brigantine, *Die Frau Metta Catharina von Flensburg*, which left their fiord for the last time in 1786.

In 1987 the diving team were rewarded for their efforts by winning the prestigious Duke of Edinburgh's Prize of the British Sub-Aqua Club. The prize was awarded for the cumulative value of the work carried out on the wreck of the *Metta Catharina* to that date. The prize was presented by His Royal Highness Prince Philip at a private ceremony in Buckingham Palace. Proud members of the winning team in attendance were Brian Bratt, Janet Chapman, Mike Evans (Senior Diver), Martin Goodson, John Greep, Colin Hannaford (Deputy Team Leader), Bob Quaye, Ian Skelton (Team Leader), and Mervyn Williams. News of the award was published in Westcountry newspapers and in an international diver's magazine.

The final accolade for the diving team was the decision by the management of the magnificent 16th century Mount Edgcumbe House, near Torpoint in Cornwall, to mount a permanent exhibition of material from the *Metta Catharina*, in a gallery overlooking the area of Plymouth Sound where the brigantine was wrecked. The exhibition, which was made possible by a generous grant from the Heritage Lottery Fund, includes all the shipboard items recovered from the wreck, together with 'Russia Calf' leather in the form of complete animal hides. The exhibition also includes interactive displays, an introductory film and outdoor activities which provide opportunities for people of all ages to learn more about the Baltic merchantman, her cargo and crew.

The Heritage Lottery Fund's Head of the South West, Nerys Watts, said of the exhibition: "international trade played an important part in the past prosperity and identity of the United Kingdom and the 18th century was the period in which Britain rose to a dominant position among European trading empires. This project provides a fascinating insight into that time and will enable people of all ages to better understand and appreciate its importance".

Members of the diving team in the Flensburg Shipping Museum in company with the Flensburg Lord Mayor and the Museum Curator. *Photo. Courtesy of the Flensburg Shipping Museum.*

Members of the diving team at Buckingham Palace with Prince Philip during the presentation to the team of the Duke of Edinburgh's Prize of the British Sub-Aqua Club. *Photo. Courtesy of Diver Magazine.*

SIXTEEN
Tanning the hides

Distinctive, aromatic, high quality 'Russia Calf' leather has for centuries been regarded as the finest in Europe. Its use by the East Asian Tartars is referred to by the ancient explorer Marco Polo and its enviable reputation had obviously spread to Genoa by the time of the wrecking of the *Metta Catharina* in 1786. The leather was known for its rich colour, its suppleness and its resistance to water. It was also reputed to be repellent to insects. All of these qualities made the leather ideal for the manufacture of boot uppers. It was also used for book-binding and for the production of fancy leather goods.

Because 'Russia Calf' leather was so highly prized, some tanneries in Europe even resorted to industrial espionage. Their spies in Tsarist Russia risked life and limb in attempts to discover all the secrets of the mysterious tanning processes, but no one ever succeeded in faithfully copying the original.

Divers examine a freshly recovered bundle of 'Russia Calf' leather. Most of the bundles contained six complete animal hides tightly rolled together. *Photo. Ian Skelton.*

Modern-day research has provided some insight into the lengthy and complex string of tanning and currying methods which placed 'Russia Calf' at the very top of every craftsman's wish-list. The pre-tanning procedure took at least six months. The actual tanning then commenced in pits filled with diluted, previously used, tanning liquid. Over a period of six or seven months the complete animal hides were turned over and over, almost continuously, by hand. They were next moved to other pits and covered with bark chippings from willow, poplar, larch or oak trees. Water was added into the mix and the hides then left to marinate for 18 months or so. After being hauled from the pits the hides were curried with seal oil and birch tar oil, dried, beaten with wood mallets, pared with a currier's shaving knife and washed.

The distinctive criss-cross grain pattern was applied while the leather was still damp. The pattern was embossed using a steel cylinder cut with many small ridges close together. The cylinder was suspended beneath a large box filled with "four hundred weight" of stones and moved back and forth across the hide using a system of ropes and pulleys. Rotating the hide through 90 degrees produced a square pattern "which pleased the public eye".

Sadly, the Russian revolution in 1917 brought an end to this mysterious age-old tanning process. 'Russia Calf' leather, it seemed, was lost to the world. How fortunate then, that in 1973 the Plymouth divers discovered the wreck of the *Metta Catharina*: a two-centuries-old time-capsule sealed during the reign of Catherine the Great. A time-capsule, which when opened, revealed a hoard of treasure. Not sparkly jewels, or pieces of eight, but tightly bound bundles of well-preserved chestnut coloured leather, swathed in grass matting. Leather, which when returned to the light of day, filled the air with a delightful smoky, oily scent. To the modern-day leather craftsman the chance to work with this treasure from 18th century Russia was a dream come true.

Large sheets of woven grass matting were used to wrap and protect the valuable bundles of Russian leather. *Photo. Ian Skelton.*

SEVENTEEN
The leather today

Cornish craftsman, Robin Snelson, first heard about the discovery of the *Metta Catharina* and her remarkable cargo, during a chance meeting with a member of the diving team in a Falmouth pub. The story of the wrecked ship prompted him to acquire an animal hide for evaluation. It was love at first sight. He was immediately attracted by the rich colour, firm texture and muted sheen of the fine 'Russia Calf' leather. He was soon in possession of more hides and after establishing a working relationship with the Plymouth divers, he was granted exclusive purchasing rights. This arrangement was by courtesy of the Duchy of Cornwall, who generously allowed the divers to sell enough of the antique leather to finance the underwater project.

Skilled Cornish leather craftsman, Robin Snelson, restores a hide from the *Metta Catharina* by applying a carefully balanced mixture of oils. *Photo. Glyn Davies.*

Traditional frame bags made by Robin Snelson. From the foreground: lady's handbag; doctor's case; barrister's bag.
Photo. Glyn Davies. Location of photo courtesy of the Sail Training Association

Although the leather had been well preserved by the deep blanket of silt at the bottom of Plymouth Sound, it was still in need of extensive conservation treatment. This was because long-term exposure to sea-water had robbed it of some of its natural oils. Despite the absence of any guidebook available for the restoration of ancient water-logged 'Russia Calf' leather, the resourceful Robin Snelson rose to the challenge. Like a latter-day alchemist he experimented over several years with exotic recipes, using ingredients such as mutton tallow, synthetic water-soluble oils, beeswax and cod oil. To this day he is still evasive when questioned about his ultimate formula. Mirroring the 18th century Russian tanners he admires so much, he jealously preserves his own hard-won 'trade secrets'.

Over the years, several other craftsmen and craftswomen have had the pleasure of working with the leather. In 1986 Robin was visited by two bespoke shoemakers from London's West End. They were fascinated by the story of the bundles of 'Russia Calf' leather, which were being recovered in Plymouth Sound from a 200 year old Danish ship. They had previously only encountered the leather in ancient book bindings. As skilled professionals they were thrilled beyond measure when, sitting in Robin's workshop, they were able to feel the texture and inhale the aromatic birch oil scent of the 18th century leather. They immediately arranged to purchase some of the very best hides for the manufacture of hand-made shoes, a pair of which were later presented to His Royal Highness Prince Charles in appreciation of his support to the Plymouth diving team.

Use of the leather has also been taken up by members of the Association of Designer Leatherworkers, an organisation founded in 1985 to share ideas and techniques within the leather-working community of Britain. Neil MacGregor of Tetbury has modified the leather in order to produce a soft, pliable by-product, which he uses to craft back-packs, gussets and soft briefcases. Other leather-workers have used hides from the *Metta Catharina* to craft field-sport equipment such as gun cases and cartridge bags. The leather has also been used for attaché, violin and doctor's cases and barrister's bags.

As a postscript to this account of 'the leather today'; in recent years a Royal Navy frigate entered Plymouth Sound and passed close to the Bridge reef before sailing up the Hamoaze to Devonport dockyard for a refit. The frigate's Captain, having heard the story of the wreck of the Baltic trader and her amazing cargo, asked if a piece of the ancient leather could be used as a writing surface for his desk. The divers were delighted to grant his wish and in due course, Ken Metcalfe, a founder member of the diving team, installed a prime section of the leather onto the desk in the Captain's cabin.

Later, when the frigate slipped her moorings, the divers took satisfaction from knowing that their gesture to the Royal Navy had brought the whole story of the *Metta Catharina* and her cargo of 'Russia Calf' leather full circle. A sample of cargo from Captain Twedt's beloved brigantine, so disastrously lost in the depths of Plymouth Sound during a stormy night in 1786, had been successfully recovered and now graced the Captain's cabin on one of Her Majesty's warships. It is tempting to imagine that as the re-commissioned HMS *Argyll* sailed proudly back out into the Sound, her Captain ventured a glance at the Bridge reef and touched his cap to a fellow seafarer.

An attaché case and a pair of bespoke shoes, hand-made from the 'Russia Calf' leather. A similar pair of shoes was presented to His Royal Highness Prince Charles in appreciation of the support he gave to the Plymouth diving team. *Photo. Glyn Davies.*

Glossary of terms

Air bags Tough, impervious, reinforced nylon bags which divers attach to heavy objects on the seabed. When filled with air the buoyant bags carry the heavy objects to the surface.

Airlift In principle the airlift is a hollow tube mounted vertically on the seabed. When air under pressure is introduced into the tube's lower end, clusters of bubbles are created, which rise rapidly up the tube. As the bubbles ascend and the water pressure around them reduces, they expand creating a powerful suction at the lower end.

Anthrax A potentially fatal disease of sheep and cattle which can be transmitted to humans.

Backstaff An instrument used by navigators to measure the angle of the sun above the horizon.

Ballast Heavy material, such as stones, which are stowed in the bottom of a ship to lower her centre of gravity and provide stability.

Bellarmine flagon A stoneware jug which has a caricatured image of Cardinal Roberto Bellarmine's face, (1542 – 1621), embossed on its neck.

Bilge The bottom of a ship's hull.

Black-out Fainting, or syncope, caused by a sudden lack of oxygen.

Bow The forward part of a ship's hull.

Bowsprit A spar projecting forward from a ship's bow.

Brig A two-masted square-rigger.

Brigantine A two-masted sailing ship, rigged square on the foremast and fore-and-aft with square topsails on the mainmast.

Bulwarks The uppermost sides of a ship.

Burst lung This often fatal disease is caused when a diver ascends holding his/her breath. The pressure build-up of air inside the lungs increases during the ascent to the point where the lungs burst causing serious injury or death.

Ceilings The internal planking of a ship's hull.

Common pump A long wood tube whose lower end rests on the ship's bottom in a compartment called the pump well. A piston and valve assembly within the tube is operated by a handle, referred to by sailors as a brake, on the upper deck of the ship to draw up and jettison unwanted water.

Coring device A small diameter sharpened steel tube, similar to an apple-corer, which is driven into contacts beneath the sea floor in order to extract small samples of material for analysis.

Currying The process of stretching and massaging tanned leather with oils in order to make it stronger and more supple.

Cutter	A wooden rowing boat sometimes referred to by sailors as a 'jolly-boat'.
Cyrillic	An alphabet used for the Russian language, named after St Cyril, (826 – 869), its reputed inventor.
Diver's marker float	A small, brightly-coloured surface buoy, which is attached to the divers by a thin line.
Fathom	A depth of six feet, (1.83 metres), of water.
Fid	A pointed hand tool used to separate strands of rope.
Firebricks	Yellow heat-resistant bricks used to line the hearth within the galley, or cookhouse.
Floors	Heavy, shaped timbers fixed to the keel at right-angles. These form the lower sections of the ribs or frames of the ship.
Forecastle	Referred to by sailors as the foc'sle, this is where the seamen's quarters are located and is situated in the bow of the ship.
Foredeck	A small raised section of deck at the bow.
Foremast	The mast closest to the ship's bow.
Galley	The ship's kitchen or cookhouse.
Gribble	A small isopod crustacean, resembling a wood louse, which attacks all sunken wood except teak.
G.R.P.	Glass reinforced plastic.
Hemp	A plant, (*Cannabis sativa*), native to Asia, used to make rope and stout fabrics.
Hove to	Come to a standstill.
Keel	The lowest longitudinal timber, which forms the backbone of a ship.
Keelson	A large longitudinal timber fixed to the tops of the floors and to the keel.
Kelp	A large plant, (*Laminaria*), with long flowing strands up to two metres long which grows in shallow water.
League	A distance of approximately three miles, (4.83 kilometres).
Lee Shore	The shore towards which the wind is blowing.
Leeward	Away from the wind.
Lifeline	A long length of pre-stretched line connecting the diver with his tender, (supervisor), in the boat. Signals are passed to and fro by a system of pulls on the line.
Mainmast	The principal mast. In a brigantine this is the second mast from the bow.
Marlinspike	See fid.
Mast-step	The rectangular shaped hole, or mortise, which is cut into the keelson to accept the lower end of the mast.

Nautical mile	A unit of approximately 2,025 yards, (1.852 kilometres).
Nitrogen	A colourless, odourless gas that forms approximately four-fifths of the earth's atmosphere. Whilst perfectly harmless to breathe on the surface, this gas can be harmful when breathed under pressure.
Nitrogen narcosis	Referred to by divers as the 'raptures of the deeps' this disease is caused by the narcotic effect of nitrogen gas under pressure in the diver's body. In extreme cases this can lead to death by drowning.
Privateer	An armed vessel owned and officered by private individuals holding a government commission and authorised for war service.
Pulley-block	A carved oval-shaped wood frame which contains one or more sheaves, (or pulley wheels). These form part of a ship's rigging and are used to lift spars and sails.
Ribs	The frames which make up the skeleton of a ship.
Salvors-in-possession	Those who have declared themselves to be the finders of the wreck.
Sheave, or shiv	A pulley wheel often made of *Lignum vitae*, a dense tropical hardwood. One or more sheaves are held inside a pulley-block by an axle or pin.
Shipworm	A mollusc which creates damaging 6 to 8 mm diameter holes and tunnels in the timbers of a ship even when the vessel is in service.
Shoal water	Shallow water.
Spars	Rounded lengths of timber including the booms and yards which hold the sails.
Stern	The rear end of a ship.
Swivel gun	A portable cannon which, when in use, was mounted on the bulwarks of a ship.
Tanning	The process of treating animal skins with tannin to make them more durable.
'The bends'	Referred to as decompression sickness, this disease is caused by bubbles of nitrogen forming within the diver's body when he/she leaves the water. A 'spinal bend', where the nitrogen bubbles affect the spine is especially serious.
Transom	A large timber which shapes and strengthens the stern of a ship.
Triangulation points	Steel tubes fixed vertically into the seabed from which measurements can be taken.
Water dredge	A long horizontal tube, mounted on the seabed, which is powered by a petrol-driven water pump on the surface. The dredge gently sucks up sediments and discharges them down-tide away from the working diver.
Water jet	A powerful jet of water, which is propelled down to the seabed, by a petrol-driven pump on the surface. The jet is used to blast away accumulations of sediment.